...you up to the
Lord today, asking
Him to give you the
strength to withstand the
blows coming from every
direction and **endure**
the storms you are facing.
I know He won't let you fall.

*We are afflicted in every way but not crushed;
we are perplexed but not in despair; we are
persecuted but not abandoned; we are
struck down but not destroyed.*

II CORINTHIANS 4:8-9 CSB

THE TRUTH IS, GOD'S STRENGTH
IS FULLY REVEALED WHEN OUR
STRENGTH IS DEPLETED.

Liz Curtis Higgs

(in)courage
A DaySpring COMMUNITY

Life can be scary at times. So today I'm praying that you can lean on the One who never fears and always loves.

There is no fear in love; instead, perfect love drives out fear.
I JOHN 4:18 CSB

BEING A WOMAN OF COURAGE LOOKS LIKE BELIEVING IN AND LEANING ON THE GOD WHO DEMOLISHES FEAR.

Anna Rendell

(in)courage

A DaySpring COMMUNITY

I am praying that God will walk right beside you in these uncertain times, guiding you every step of the way. May you trust Him through the entire journey.

For I am the LORD your God, who holds your right hand, who says to you, "Do not fear, I will help you."
ISAIAH 41:13 CSB

FAITH IS TAKING THE FIRST STEP EVEN WHEN YOU DON'T SEE THE WHOLE STAIRCASE.

Martin Luther King Jr.

(in)courage
A DaySpring COMMUNITY

God will never let you go. Never! I pray you remember that and trust Him, no matter how dark your days.

Do not fear, for I am with you;
do not be afraid, for I am your God.
I will strengthen you; I will help you;
I will hold on to you with My
righteous right hand.

ISAIAH 41:10 CSB

FAITH IS NOT MERELY HOLDING ON TO GOD.
IT IS GOD HOLDING ON TO YOU.

Corrie ten Boom

(in)courage

A DaySpring COMMUNITY

I am praying that you don't let today's disappointments take tomorrow's victories hostage. Trust in the Lord and His timing—and His promise to never leave you and always be there for you.

Let us not become weary in doing good, for at the proper time we will reap a harvest if we do not give up.

GALATIANS 6:9 NIV

COURAGE DOESN'T ALWAYS ROAR. SOMETIMES COURAGE IS THE QUIET VOICE AT THE END OF THE DAY SAYING, "I WILL TRY AGAIN TOMORROW."

Mary Anne Radmacher

I'm praying that the Lord gives you the words you need, when you need them. May He give you both courage and compassion for the conversations you have with the people in your life.

The wicked flee when no one is pursuing them, but the righteous are as bold as a lion.

PROVERBS 28:1 CSB

LET US NOT SHY AWAY FROM BEING BOLD FOR CHRIST, AND MAY OUR BOLDNESS BE COUPLED WITH LOVE.

Michelle Reyes

(in)courage
A DaySpring COMMUNITY

Your time in the wilderness will not last forever, and it will not be in vain. I'm praying for God to give you clarity during this confusing time.

Moses answered the people, "Do not be afraid. Stand firm and you will see the deliverance the LORD will bring you today. The Egyptians you see today you will never see again."

EXODUS 14:13 NIV

TAKE COURAGE. WE WALK IN THE WILDERNESS TODAY AND IN THE PROMISED LAND TOMORROW.

D. L. Moody

(in)courage

A DaySpring COMMUNITY

My prayer for you is wild adventure as you follow the Lord's call with abandon, letting loose of every fear or worry that ties you down and instead flying into the beautiful future that He has planned.

Let us run with endurance the race that lies before us, keeping our eyes on Jesus, the Source and Perfecter of our faith.

HEBREWS 12:1-2 CSB

A SHIP IS SAFE IN HARBOR,
BUT THAT'S NOT WHAT SHIPS ARE FOR.

William G. T. Shedd

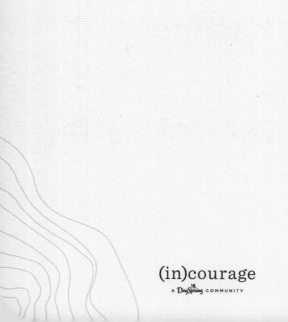

You are doing the Lord's work, and He will give you what you need to finish it. I pray you can take small steps forward and then watch God turn your fishes and loaves into a feast!

Therefore, my dear brothers and sisters, stand firm. Let nothing move you. Always give yourselves fully to the work of the Lord, because you know that your labor in the Lord is not in vain.

I CORINTHIANS 15:58 NIV

IF GOD WANTS A THING TO SUCCEED, YOU CAN'T MESS IT UP. IF HE WANTS A THING TO FAIL, YOU CAN'T SAVE IT. REST AND JUST BE FAITHFUL.

Jennie Allen

(in)courage

A DaySpring COMMUNITY

I am praying for you today—that you **remember** how much our mighty God **loves** you and how He will never leave you. **Have courage!** He's with you every step of the way.

The LORD Himself goes before you and will be with you; He will never leave you nor forsake you. Do not be afraid; do not be discouraged.
DEUTERONOMY 31:8 NIV

NOTHING CAN DEFEAT OUR GOD WHO CARES DEEPLY ABOUT YOU. HE WILL NEVER LEAVE YOU ALONE; HE WILL BE WITH YOU WHEREVER YOU GO (NO MATTER HOW DARK IT GETS).

Mary Carver

(in)courage
A DaySpring COMMUNITY

Though your situation seems **hopeless,** I pray you hold fast to your **hope** in the Lord. May your trust in **His love** and in His plans for you grow even **stronger** during these difficult times.

May the God of hope fill you with all joy and peace as you trust in Him, so that you may overflow with hope by the power of the Holy Spirit.

ROMANS 15:13 NIV

GOD IS WHISPERING WORDS OF HOPE AND LIGHT IN THE MIDST OF WHAT APPEARS TO BE DARK.

Bonnie Gray

(in)courage
A DaySpring COMMUNITY

Doing the right thing is not always easy. I pray that His strength and courage will be more than enough to help you stand for what is right and good in His sight.

Therefore, put on every piece of God's armor so you will be able to resist the enemy in the time of evil. Then after the battle you will still be standing firm.
EPHESIANS 6:13 NLT

IT TAKES A GREAT DEAL OF BRAVERY
TO STAND UP TO OUR ENEMIES—
BUT JUST AS MUCH TO STAND UP
TO OUR FRIENDS.

J. K. Rowling

(in)courage
A DaySpring COMMUNITY

I am asking God to give you strength and courage today. Though your circumstances may not change, I'm praying that your heart is encouraged by knowing He is with you.

Have I not commanded you? Be strong and courageous. Do not be afraid; do not be discouraged, for the LORD your God will be with you wherever you go.

JOSHUA 1:9 NIV

GOD RARELY MAKES OUR FEAR DISAPPEAR.
INSTEAD, HE ASKS US TO BE STRONG
AND TAKE TO COURAGE.

Bruce Wilkinson

(in)courage

A *DaySpring* COMMUNITY

May you take comfort and courage in the knowledge that the God who created the universe also created you and loves you more than you can understand.

He determines the number of the stars and calls them each by name. Great is our Lord and mighty in power; His understanding has no limit.
PSALM 147:4-5 NIV

REST ASSURED, THE SAME ONE WHO HOLDS THE STARS AND PLANETS IN SPACE CAN TAKE CARE OF YOU.

Edie Emory

(in)courage
A DaySpring COMMUNITY

I am praying that you would feel surrounded by love and friendship today, that God would bless you with rewarding relationships and a caring community.

Get rid of all bitterness, rage and anger, brawling and slander, along with every form of malice. Be kind and compassionate to one another, forgiving each other, just as in Christ God forgave you.

EPHESIANS 4:31-32 NIV

TO LOVE AT ALL IS TO BE VULNERABLE.

C. S. Lewis

(in)courage

A *DaySpring* COMMUNITY

I am praying for God to give you strength, courage, and peace of mind today. I'm asking Him to help you remember that He is with you no matter how hard life is or how scared you are.

*But those who trust in the L*ORD *will find new strength. They will soar high on wings like eagles. They will run and not grow weary. They will walk and not faint.*
ISAIAH 40:31 NLT

THE JOURNEY OF FAITH MAY BE
FULL OF UNKNOWNS, BUT WITH JESUS,
YOU'LL DISCOVER THAT THOUGH
THE WATERS RAGE, YOU WILL ALWAYS
RISE ABOVE.

Lauren Gaskill

I am praying that you take one day at a time, make one step at a time, in this overwhelming season, trusting God and leaning on the strength and courage He promises all along the way.

Therefore don't worry about tomorrow, because tomorrow will worry about itself. Each day has enough trouble of its own.

MATTHEW 6:34 CSB

COURAGE IS MORE EXHILARATING THAN FEAR, AND IN THE LONG RUN IT IS EASIER. WE DO NOT HAVE TO BECOME HEROES OVERNIGHT. JUST A STEP AT A TIME, MEETING EACH THING THAT COMES UP, SEEING IT IS NOT AS DREADFUL AS IT APPEARED, DISCOVERING WE HAVE THE STRENGTH TO STARE IT DOWN.

Eleanor Roosevelt

(in)courage
A DaySpring COMMUNITY

God can do anything!
And today I'm praying
you remember that, no
matter how difficult life is
or how scary the future.
I pray He gives you courage
as you face what comes
next with Him.

Be strong and courageous. Do not be afraid or
terrified because of them, for the LORD your
God goes with you; He will never leave you
nor forsake you.
DEUTERONOMY 31:6 NIV

DO NOT LIMIT THE LIMITLESS GOD!
WITH HIM, FACE THE FUTURE
UNAFRAID BECAUSE YOU ARE
NEVER ALONE.

Lettie Cowman

(in)courage

A *DaySpring* COMMUNITY

I am asking God
to keep you mindful of
His faithfulness today,
so that you can remain
steadfast and strong
despite your fears.

*You will keep in perfect peace
those whose minds are steadfast,
because they trust in You.*

ISAIAH 26:3 NIV

I LEARNED THAT COURAGE WAS
NOT THE ABSENCE OF FEAR, BUT
THE TRIUMPH OVER IT. THE BRAVE
MAN IS NOT HE WHO DOES NOT
FEEL AFRAID, BUT HE WHO
CONQUERS THAT FEAR.

Nelson Mandela

(in)courage
A DaySpring COMMUNITY

God wants to redeem the areas of our lives where we've been hurt. I just wanted to let you know, I'm here for you. You can trust me with your pain.

"Go," said Jesus, "your faith has healed you." Immediately he received his sight and followed Jesus along the road.

MARK 10:52 NIV

WHEN WE NAME OUR PAIN AND TELL OUR STORY TO SOMEONE TRUSTWORTHY, HEALING BEGINS ITS SLOW, DEEP WORK WITHIN US, ALLOWING THE LIGHT TO SEEP IN WHERE DARKNESS WAS BEFORE.

Aliza Latta

(in)courage
A DaySpring COMMUNITY

I am praying for you today, asking the Lord to strengthen your faith in His mighty power and never-changing love.

For I the LORD do not change; therefore you, O children of Jacob, are not consumed.

MALACHI 3:6 ESV

NEVER FORGET THAT GOD ISN'T BOUND BY TIME THE WAY WE ARE. WE ONLY SEE THE PRESENT MOMENT; GOD SEES EVERYTHING. WE SEE ONLY PART OF WHAT HE IS DOING; HE SEES IT ALL.

Billy Graham

(in)courage

A DaySpring COMMUNITY

I am praying that when you look in the mirror, you see the strong warrior God has created you to be. Lean on His strength and trust who He says you are.

My health may fail, and my spirit may grow weak, but God remains the strength of my heart; He is mine forever.
PSALM 73:26 NLT

WE ARE WILD WARRIORS WHEN WE REALIZE THAT WE ARE STRONGER AND BRAVER THAN WE'VE YET TO SEE— BECAUSE THEN WE STOP COWERING AND START SWINGING OUR SWORDS.

Holley Gerth

(in)courage
A DaySpring COMMUNITY

I am asking God to build your trust in Him even when your world is falling apart. May He renew your hope and strength as you face this difficult situation.

So be strong and courageous, all you who put your hope in the LORD!

PSALM 31:24 NLT

GOD CHOOSES TO HARVEST HOPE IN THE MIDST OF WILD UNCERTAINTY AND DEEP HEARTACHE.

Jenny Howell

(in)courage
A DaySpring COMMUNITY

I am praying that you choose courage. Choose brave, choose bold, choose walking in faith even when you cannot see the way. God will show you the way and walk with you in it.

Be strong and courageous, because you will lead these people to inherit the land I swore to their ancestors to give them.

JOSHUA 1:6 NIV

YOU CAN CHOOSE COURAGE
OR YOU CAN CHOOSE COMFORT,
BUT YOU CANNOT CHOOSE BOTH.

Brene Brown

(in)courage
A DaySpring COMMUNITY

God doesn't ask us to be smarter or faster or stronger or better. I'm praying He will free your mind of any unrealistic expectations that cause you stress and worry.

For I can do everything through Christ, who gives me strength.

PHILIPPIANS 4:13 NLT

GOD USES ORDINARY PEOPLE WHO ARE OBEDIENT TO HIM TO DO EXTRAORDINARY THINGS.

John Maxwell

God is good, and He loves you more than you can imagine. No matter what comes your way, I'm praying that you remember those truths and face it with **courage** and **strength.**

The LORD is good, a stronghold in a day of distress; He cares for those who take refuge in Him.

NAHUM 1:7 CSB

IF THE LORD BE WITH US, WE HAVE NO CAUSE FOR FEAR. HIS EYE IS UPON US, HIS ARM OVER US, HIS EAR OPEN TO OUR PRAYER—HIS GRACE SUFFICIENT, HIS PROMISE UNCHANGEABLE.

John Newton

You've got this. Not because you're strong enough, but because God is and He is fighting for you. I believe in you because I believe in Him. I pray you remember that today.

Be strong, and let us fight bravely for our people and the cities of our God. The LORD will do what is good in His sight.

I CHRONICLES 19:13 NIV

IN EVERY BATTLE WE FACE, VICTORY IS ALREADY OURS IN CHRIST.

Stephanie Bryant

I know you might be worried, nervous, or scared right now. I'm praying for you, lifting you up to the Lord and asking Him to comfort and protect you.

Do not be anxious about anything, but in every situation, by prayer and petition, with thanksgiving, present your requests to God.

PHILIPPIANS 4:6 NIV

**REPLACE WORRY WITH PRAYER.
MAKE THE DECISION TO PRAY WHENEVER
YOU CATCH YOURSELF WORRYING.**

Elizabeth George

You were made for more than an average, lukewarm life. I'm praying you find the **courage** and **strength** to follow God into the astonishing, spectacular story He's written for you!

"But because You say so, I will let down the nets." When they had done so, they caught such a large number of fish that their nets began to break.

LUKE 5:5-6 NIV

DO NOT BE AFRAID. DO NOT BE SATISFIED WITH MEDIOCRITY. PUT OUT INTO THE DEEP AND LET DOWN YOUR NETS FOR A CATCH.

Pope John Paul II

Even though we can't see it, **God is always working all things together for our good and His glory.** I'm praying you remember that God has already won the war.

"Do not be afraid of them," the LORD said to Joshua, "for I have given you victory over them. Not a single one of them will be able to stand up to you."

JOSHUA 10:8 NLT

WHEN IT LOOKS LIKE THINGS ARE OUT OF CONTROL, BEHIND THE SCENES THERE IS A GOD WHO HAS NOT SURRENDERED AUTHORITY.

A. W. Tozer

(in)courage

A DaySpring COMMUNITY

Aren't you glad to know that God is on your side? I am—and I'm asking Him to give you courage as you remember that He will fight your battles for you, that He will always win.

Though a mighty army surrounds me, my heart will not be afraid. Even if I am attacked, I will remain confident.

PSALM 27:3 NLT

THIS THING THAT HAS BECOME YOUR PERSONAL DEMON, YOUR CURSE, YOUR BATTLEFIELD? I PROMISE YOU IT IS NOT BIGGER THAN OUR GOD, AND IT IS NOT STRONGER THAN HIS LOVE FOR YOU.

Mary Carver

(in)courage
A DaySpring COMMUNITY

God has tremendous plans for you, and none of them include worry and fear. I'm praying that you place your hope in His good plans for you and your life today.

"For I know the plans I have for you," *declares the* Lord, *"plans to prosper you* *and not to harm you, plans to give you* *hope and a future."*

JEREMIAH 29:11 NIV

THE WONDERFUL TRUTH IS THAT WORRY AND FEAR ARE NOT PART OF HIS PLAN FOR US.

Jennifer Ueckert

I am asking God to open your eyes to every single thing that could give you courage in your journey. May His encouraging ways be surprising and delightful today!

Now the brothers and sisters from there had heard the news about us and had come to meet us as far as the Forum of Appius and the Three Taverns. When Paul saw them, he thanked God and took courage.

ACTS 28:15 CSB

COURAGE IS FOUND IN UNLIKELY PLACES.

J. R. R. Tolkien

(in)courage

A DaySpring COMMUNITY

I am praying you feel God's presence today, **trusting that He is with you** wherever you go and in whatever challenges you face. He will never leave you.

For I am convinced that neither death nor life, neither angels nor demons, neither the present nor the future, nor any powers, neither height nor depth, nor anything else in all creation, will be able to separate us from the love of God that is in Christ Jesus our Lord.

ROMANS 8:38-39 NIV

FAITH IS NOT BELIEVING IN MY OWN UNSHAKABLE BELIEF. FAITH IS BELIEVING IN AN UNSHAKABLE GOD WHEN EVERYTHING IN ME TREMBLES AND QUAKES.

Beth Moore

(in)courage

A DaySpring COMMUNITY

My prayer for you is that you not grow weary as you step forward in courage and lean on God's strength again and again. I pray you remember that He's always with you.

I am sure of this, that He who started a good work in you will carry it on to completion until the day of Christ Jesus.

PHILIPPIANS 1:6 CSB

COURAGE IS VERY IMPORTANT. LIKE A MUSCLE, IT IS STRENGTHENED BY USE.

Ruth Gordon

(in)courage

A DaySpring COMMUNITY

Trusting God and leaning on His strength means that you can face anything life throws at you. I pray you feel secure in His protection and the freedom found only in His promises.

Therefore put on the full armor of God, so that when the day of evil comes, you may be able to stand your ground, and after you have done everything, to stand.

EPHESIANS 6:13 NIV

KNOWING THAT YOUR FUTURE IS ABSOLUTELY ASSURED CAN FREE YOU TO LIVE ABUNDANTLY TODAY.

Sarah Young

What you're facing is hard, but you aren't alone! God has given us the Holy Spirit, and I'm praying He comforts and guides you during this season.

The Spirit of God, who raised Jesus from the dead, lives in you. And just as God raised Christ Jesus from the dead, He will give life to your mortal bodies by this same Spirit living within you.

ROMANS 8:11 NLT

IN CHRIST, YOU ARE NEVER ALONE.
HIS SPIRIT LIVES IN YOU.

Denise Hughes

(in)courage
A DaySpring COMMUNITY

I am praying you see yourself the way God sees you—beautiful, smart, and strong. Take heart! May that knowledge give you the courage to do the good works He's prepared for you.

For we are God's handiwork, created in Christ Jesus to do good works, which God prepared in advance for us to do.

EPHESIANS 2:10 NIV

IT TAKES COURAGE TO GROW UP AND BECOME WHO YOU REALLY ARE.

E. E. Cummings

(in)courage
A DaySpring COMMUNITY

I'm thanking God today for the ability to pray our way through life's storms. And I'm asking Him to make His love and presence known when you bring your own troubles to Him.

Do not be anxious about anything, but in every situation, by prayer and petition, with thanksgiving, present your requests to God.

PHILIPPIANS 4:6 NIV

WHEN WE CHOOSE THANKFUL PRAYER OVER WALLOWING IN ANXIETY AND WORRY, WE ARE DEMONSTRATING AN UNWAVERING TRUST IN GOD.

Priscilla Shirer

(in)courage
A DaySpring COMMUNITY

I am praying God gives you the courage to keep loving others, even when you're hurt and disappointed.

For God has not given us a spirit of fear, but one of power, love, and sound judgment.
II TIMOTHY 1:7 CSB

HAVE ENOUGH COURAGE TO TRUST LOVE ONE MORE TIME AND ALWAYS ONE MORE TIME.

Maya Angelou

(in)courage
A DaySpring COMMUNITY

I believe that God has a specific purpose for you in the exact place you are today. I'm praying He reveals it to you and gives you the courage to follow His plan.

Who knows, perhaps you have come to your royal position for such a time as this.
ESTHER 4:14 CSB

GOD IS THE HERO OF THIS STORY, NOT ME. HE SPOKE THE WORD, HE PUT ME ON THE PATH, AND HE WILL KEEP ME FROM WANDERING OFF THE PATH.

Christie Thomas

God will never, ever let you down, and I'm praying you hold tightly to that truth while you radically release your fears and doubts and anxieties.

Let us hold unswervingly to the hope we profess, for He who promised is faithful.
HEBREWS 10:23 NIV

TRUE FAITH MEANS HOLDING NOTHING BACK. IT MEANS PUTTING EVERY HOPE IN GOD'S FIDELITY TO HIS PROMISES.

Francis Chan

This world will always bring us trouble, but God promises us we are **never alone.** I'm praying that you feel His presence and His **strength** while you walk through this storm.

When you pass through the waters, I will be with you; and when you pass through the rivers, they will not sweep over you. When you walk through the fire, you will not be burned; the flames will not set you ablaze.

ISAIAH 43:2 NIV

FAITH DOES NOT LIE IN TRUSTING GOD TO STOP THE STORM, BUT IN TRUSTING HIM TO ENABLE US TO WALK THROUGH THE STORM.

Jill Briscoe

I am praying for God to reveal His love and power to you today. He will protect you and He will never, ever leave you.

Every word of God proves true; he is a shield to those who take refuge in him.

PROVERBS 30:5 ESV

THE WAY TO STOP UNRAVELING INTO THE FEAR IS BY FOLDING MYSELF INTO THE GOSPEL.

Kristen Strong

(in)courage
A DaySpring COMMUNITY

My heart hurts for you today, and I'm praying that God comforts you and gives you the courage to go on to grow in strength and faith.

Consider it pure joy, my brothers and sisters, whenever you face trials of many kinds, because you know that the testing of your faith produces perseverance. Let perseverance finish its work so that you may be mature and complete, not lacking anything.

JAMES 1:2-4 NIV

TAKE CHANCES; MAKE MISTAKES. THAT'S HOW YOU GROW. PAIN NOURISHES YOUR COURAGE. YOU HAVE TO FAIL IN ORDER TO PRACTICE BEING BRAVE.

Mary Tyler Moore

Life can be so heavy. But you don't have to carry all your cares alone! Praying you lean on God and let Him lighten your load today.

Come to me, all of you who are weary and burdened, and I will give you rest.
MATTHEW 11:28 CSB

NO MAN EVER SANK UNDER THE BURDEN OF THE DAY. IT IS WHEN TOMORROW'S BURDEN IS ADDED TO THE BURDEN OF TODAY THAT THE WEIGHT IS MORE THAN A MAN CAN BEAR. NEVER LOAD YOURSELF SO.

George MacDonald

I am praying that God will reveal His heart to you so you know without a doubt how much He loves and cares for you.

Surely God is my salvation;
I will trust and not be afraid.
The LORD, the LORD himself,
is my strength and my defense;
He has become my salvation.

ISAIAH 12:2 NIV

BLESS US, FATHER, EVEN IN
OUR LACK OF TRUST, AND DRAW
US CLOSE TO YOU.

Rachel Hammond

It is okay to admit that you need help. I pray you are brave enough to share your struggles—and that God's strength can then speak volumes to you and to those around you.

[God] said, "My grace is all you need. My power works best in weakness." So now I am glad to boast about my weaknesses, so that the power of Christ can work through me.... For when I am weak, then I am strong.

II CORINTHIANS 12:9-10 NLT

GOD'S POWER SHOWS UP IN OUR WEAKNESS WHEN WE'RE WILLING TO BE REAL ABOUT OUR STRUGGLES AND OUR NEED FOR HIS STRENGTH.

Renee Swope

(in)courage

A DaySpring COMMUNITY

Looking at the whole journey can be overwhelming, so I'm praying that you can take one step at a time. May the Lord guide you and give you just what you need for today.

Let me hear of your unfailing love each morning, for I am trusting you. Show me where to walk, for I give myself to you.

PSALM 143:8 NLT

FAITH DOES NOT CONCERN ITSELF
WITH THE ENTIRE JOURNEY.
ONE STEP IS ENOUGH.

Lettie Cowman

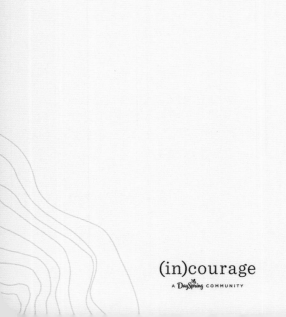

I love how **you defend** those who cannot defend themselves. I'm praying God continues to give you astonishing amounts of **courage** to do His work.

There is no greater love than to lay down one's life for one's friends.
JOHN 15:13 NLT

WE BELIEVE IN ORDINARY ACTS OF BRAVERY, IN THE COURAGE THAT DRIVES ONE PERSON TO STAND UP FOR ANOTHER.

Veronica Roth

I know it's hard to wait, but it will be worth it. God's timing is always so much better than ours, and I'm praying He gives you the patience and strength to trust and wait on Him.

Wait patiently for the LORD.
Be brave and courageous.
Yes, wait patiently for the LORD.

PSALM 27:14 NLT

GOD'S TIMING IS
ALWAYS PERFECT.
TRUST HIS DELAYS.
HE'S GOT YOU.

Tony Evans

What is God calling you to do today? Simply focus on the first step and take it, knowing He's right beside you. That is my prayer for you.

I tell you the truth, if you had faith even as small as a mustard seed, you could say to this mountain, "Move from here to there," and it would move. Nothing would be impossible.
MATTHEW 17:20 NLT

SMALL ACTS OF FAITH
MATTER IN BIG WAYS.

Mary Carver

I know how tempting
it is to fight back,
to defend yourself, but I'm
asking God to do that for
you. I'm praying He gives
you peace of mind and
heart while He fights
your every battle.

The LORD will fight for you;
you need only to be still.
EXODUS 14:14 NIV

REMEMBER, NO MATTER WHAT YOUR
BATTLE IS, IT IS NOT YOURS; THE BATTLE
BELONGS TO THE LORD, AND HE HAS A
PLAN TO BRING YOU VICTORY.

Joyce Meyer

I am praying that you listen only to the voice of God today, that **He blocks any lies** coming your way and that you remain **strong** and **steady** in the **Truth.**

It is better to take refuge in the LORD than to trust in people.

PSALM 118:8 NLT

WHATEVER YOU DO, YOU NEED COURAGE. WHATEVER COURSE YOU DECIDE UPON, THERE IS ALWAYS SOMEONE TO TELL YOU THAT YOU ARE WRONG. THERE ARE ALWAYS DIFFICULTIES ARISING THAT TEMPT YOU TO BELIEVE YOUR CRITICS ARE RIGHT.

Ralph Waldo Emerson

(in)courage
A DaySpring COMMUNITY

Let us thank God for the trials He has allowed in our lives, building our **character and faith.** Let us wait on His timing, **trusting** Him to hold us and mold us through it all.

Consider it a great joy, my brothers and sisters, whenever you experience various trials, because you know that the testing of your faith produces endurance.

JAMES 1:2-3 CSB

THE DEEPEST SPIRITUAL LESSONS ARE NOT LEARNED BY HIS LETTING US HAVE OUR WAY IN THE END, BUT BY HIS MAKING US WAIT, BEARING WITH US IN LOVE AND PATIENCE UNTIL WEARE ABLE TO HONESTLY PRAY WHAT HE TAUGHT HIS DISCIPLES TO PRAY: THY WILL BE DONE.

Elisabeth Elliot

(in)courage
A DaySpring COMMUNITY

Praying you are surrounded by uplifting words that soothe and sustain your soul. May God protect you from lies and use loving truth to give you strength.

Kind words are like honey—sweet to the soul and healthy for the body.
PROVERBS 16:24 NLT

WHILE SHAMING WORDS CAN TAKE COURAGE OUT OF A SOUL, ENCOURAGING AND AFFIRMING WORDS CAN PUT COURAGE BACK IN.

Scott Sauls

(in)courage

A DaySpring COMMUNITY

Fear can force us to rush, to worry, to wonder why everything is taking so long. I'm praying you rest in the comfort of knowing that God's timing is always the perfect rhythm for our lives.

"For I know the plans I have for you," declares the LORD, "plans to prosper you and not to harm you, plans to give you hope and a future."

JEREMIAH 29:11 NIV

IT TAKES COURAGE TO LISTEN WITH OUR WHOLE HEART TO THE TICK OF GOD'S TIMING, RATHER THAN MARCH TO THE BEAT OF OUR FEARS.

Ann Voskamp

(in)courage
A DaySpring COMMUNITY

When you've got **God on your side** **(and you do!), nothing is impossible.** No matter the obstacles you face or how scared you feel, God works in and through you. I'm praying you remember that today.

Then David said, "The LORD who rescued me from the paw of the lion and the paw of the bear will rescue me from the hand of this Philistine." Saul said to David, "Go, and may the LORD be with you."

I SAMUEL 17:37 CSB

STOP SAYING YOU'RE TOO SCARED. STOP HIDING. STOP SAYING THERE'S NO WAY FOR YOU. LOOK BACK ON ALL YOU'VE DONE. YOUR HISTORY TELLS ANOTHER STORY.

Jennifer Dukes Lee

I pray you have the **courage to stand firm** no matter how impossible the situation seems. I pray God will help you **keep going** even when you want to quit. I pray you **persevere** to the end.

Blessed is the one who perseveres under trial because, having stood the test, that person will receive the crown of life that the Lord has promised to those who love Him.

JAMES 1:12 NIV

[COURAGE IS] WHEN YOU KNOW YOU'RE LICKED BEFORE YOU BEGIN, BUT YOU BEGIN ANYWAY AND SEE IT THROUGH NO MATTER WHAT.

Atticus Finch,
To Kill a Mockingbird

(in)courage
A DaySpring COMMUNITY

You are so very loved, and I'm asking God to make that known to your soul. I pray that you feel His love and it gives you courage to face whatever comes your way.

"Don't be afraid," He said, "for you are very precious to God. Peace! Be encouraged! Be strong!"
DANIEL 10:19 NLT

COURAGE COMES FROM A HEART
THAT IS CONVINCED IT IS LOVED.

Beth Moore

(in)courage

A DaySpring COMMUNITY

Standing for what's right can be a lonely place. Today I'm praying God wraps you in His arms and reminds you that you are never alone; He is always with you.

Fear of man will prove to be a snare, but whoever trusts in the LORD is kept safe.
PROVERBS 29:25 NIV

YOU MUST NEVER BE FEARFUL ABOUT WHAT YOU ARE DOING WHEN IT'S RIGHT.

Rosa Parks

You can do this! I believe in you, and I believe in God. I'm praying that He gives you wings as you take this leap to follow Him.

Jesus looked at them and said, "With man this is impossible, but with God all things are possible."
MATTHEW 19:26 NIV

DREAMS ARE AUDACIOUS, HOPE-WINGED LEAPS INSPIRED BY A FUTURE THAT AWAITS US. DREAMING TAKES COURAGE!

Lucretia Berry

(in)courage
A DaySpring COMMUNITY

Fear is not in charge! The world cannot win this battle! God is **all-knowing** and **all-powerful,** and He loves you so much that He is **fighting** on your behalf. I pray you are **strengthened** to know that.

I have told you these things, so that in Me you may have peace. In this world you will have trouble. But take heart!
I have overcome the world.

JOHN 16:33 NIV

COURAGE ISN'T THE ABSENCE OF FEAR; IT'S JUST DECIDING THAT FEAR ISN'T CALLING THE SHOTS ANYMORE.

Bob Goff

I am praying that the Lord hears your cry and goes before you to face your enemy. May you rest in the knowledge that He hears your every prayer and fights your every battle.

We have the LORD our God to help us and to fight our battles.
II CHRONICLES 32:8 CSB

IN PRAYER YOU GAIN YOUR STRENGTH—THE POWER TO GIRD YOURSELF WITH ARMOR THAT EXTINGUISHES EVERY WEAPON YOUR ENEMY WIELDS.

Priscilla Shirer

Don't be ashamed when you cry to God for help. He is always there, waiting for you and wanting to hold you and help you. I pray you find comfort in His arms.

In my distress I called to the LORD;
I cried to my God for help. From His
temple He heard my voice; my cry came
before Him, into His ears.

PSALM 18:6 NIV

COURAGE IS FOR ALL OF US WHO
ADMIT HOW SCARED WE ARE AND PUT
OUR FLAILING SELVES INTO THE EVER-
OUTSTRETCHED HANDS OF JESUS.

Tasha Jun

(in)courage
A DaySpring COMMUNITY

I am praying that you **trust** the Lord during this season. He has **big things** ahead for you!

You will keep in perfect peace those whose minds are steadfast, because they trust in You. Trust in the Lord forever, for the Lord, the Lord Himself, is the Rock eternal.

ISAIAH 26:3-4 NIV

YOU CANNOT SWIM FOR NEW
HORIZONS UNTIL YOU HAVE
COURAGE TO LOSE SIGHT OF THE SHORE.

William Faulkner

(in)courage
A DaySpring COMMUNITY

I am asking the Lord to help you figure out what to do—and I know He will do it. He has the answers you need, and He will guide you along the way.

Commit everything you do to the LORD. Trust Him, and He will help you.

PSALM 37:5 NLT

JESUS GIVES US HOPE BECAUSE HE KEEPS US COMPANY, HAS A VISION, AND KNOWS THE WAY WE SHOULD GO.

Max Lucado

(in)courage
A DaySpring COMMUNITY

Even when your future feels unknown, God is writing your story. I'm praying He will guide you through every plot twist and new chapter until He reveals the incredible ending.

"Now this is what the LORD says—the One who created you, Jacob, and the One who formed you, Israel—"Do not fear, for I have redeemed you; I have called you by your name; you are Mine."

ISAIAH 43:1 CSB

WE MAY NOT KNOW WHAT THE FUTURE HOLDS, BUT WE CAN TRUST THE AUTHOR WITH OUR STORY'S ENDING.

Lori Schumaker

I am asking God to give you courage and strength today. I'm asking Him to make Himself known in your life as He answers your every request and gives you exactly what you need.

Have I not commanded you? Be strong and courageous. Do not be afraid; do not be discouraged, for the LORD your God will be with you wherever you go.

JOSHUA 1:9 NIV

HE IS WITH YOU IN THE MIDST OF YOUR STRUGGLE. HE WILL CARE FOR YOU, AND HE WILL MAKE HIMSELF GREAT IN YOUR LIFE.

Michelle Reyes

(in)courage
A DaySpring COMMUNITY

Even when the odds seem stacked against you and you can't see God at work, He hasn't left you alone. Today I pray that you find strength in knowing He is always with you.

When He is at work in the north, I do not see Him; when He turns to the south, I catch no glimpse of Him. But He knows the way that I take; when He has tested me, I will come forth as gold. My feet have closely followed His steps; I have kept to His way without turning aside.

JOB 23:9-11 NIV

JUST BECAUSE YOU CAN'T SEE THE WAY DOESN'T MEAN THAT GOD DOESN'T HAVE THE WAY. WALK IN FAITH.

Tony Evans

(in)courage

A *DaySpring* COMMUNITY

I am praying that God fills your **cup to overflowing** with the **courage** you need to **hope** in Him and **trust** Him for your every need.

May the God of hope fill you with all joy and peace as you trust in Him, so that you may overflow with hope by the power of the Holy Spirit.

ROMANS 15:13 NIV

MAY YOUR CHOICES REFLECT YOUR HOPES, NOT YOUR FEARS.

Nelson Mandela

I am praying that God helps you see yourself the way He sees you, to know how capable you are of succeeding and to believe without a doubt that He loves you endlessly.

"No weapon formed against you will succeed, and you will refute any accusation raised against you in court. This is the heritage of the LORD'S servants, and their vindication is from me." This is the LORD'S declaration.

ISAIAH 54:17 CSB

HOLY CONFIDENCE IS AN ACT OF WAR AGAINST THE ENEMY OF OUR HEART.

Holley Gerth

(in)courage
A DaySpring COMMUNITY

I am praying God gives you the courage to believe in Him today, to believe that He can and will do what He's promised, to believe He loves you enough to make it all true.

The LORD is my strength and my shield;
my heart trusts in Him, and I am helped.
Therefore my heart celebrates, and I give
thanks to Him with my song.

PSALM 28:7 CSB

DARE TO HOPE THAT GOD IS
WHO HE SAYS HE IS, THAT HE'LL
DO WHAT HE SAYS HE'LL DO.

Mary Carver

(in)courage
A DaySpring COMMUNITY

Though this storm is scary, I'm praying He will **keep you from drowning** and **pull you out of the water.**

When the disciples saw Him walking on the sea, they were terrified. "It's a ghost!" they said, and they cried out in fear. Immediately Jesus spoke to them. "Have courage! It is I. Don't be afraid."

MATTHEW 14:26-27 CSB

THE ONLY WAY TO STAY ABOVE THE WATER IS TO TRUST THE ONE WHO WALKED ON THE WAVES.

Anna Rendell

(in)courage
A DaySpring COMMUNITY

You are an **incredible masterpiece,** created by the Lord God Himself. I pray that gives you **courage** to be the **extraordinary** person He made you to be.

I will praise you because I have been remarkably and wondrously made. Your works are wondrous, and I know this very well.

PSALM 139:14 CSB

THE THING THAT IS REALLY HARD, AND REALLY AMAZING, IS GIVING UP ON BEING PERFECT AND BEGINNING THE WORK OF BECOMING YOURSELF.

Anna Quindlen

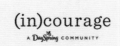
(in)courage
A DaySpring COMMUNITY

Today I'm praying you remember this–the same God who spoke this world into existence also loves you, will strengthen you, and will never, ever leave you.

The LORD merely spoke, and the heavens were created. He breathed the word, and all the stars were born.... For when He spoke, the world began! It appeared at His command.
PSALM 33:6,9 NLT

WHEN THE WORLD CAREENS OUT OF CONTROL, WE CAN REST IN THE FACT THAT GOD SPUN THIS WORLD WITH A SIMPLE WORD.

Mary DeMuth

Tomorrow is daunting, the Lord understands that. He's already there, making a way for you. I'm praying you rest in the knowledge that your future is secure in His hands.

"I am the Alpha and the Omega," says the Lord God, "the One Who is, Who was, and Who is to come, the Almighty."
REVELATION 1:8 CSB

I AM ENCOURAGED THAT THERE IS HOPE IN THE FACE OF THE UNKNOWN, AND THAT I DON'T HAVE TO WORRY ABOUT TOMORROW BECAUSE HE IS ALREADY THERE.

Amy Lathrop

I am praying you step boldly into the future God has planned for you, trusting that He is right there beside you, holding you, guiding you, and protecting you.

I know the LORD is always with me. I will not be shaken, for He is right beside me.
PSALM 16:8 NLT

WHEN WE FACE OUR FEARS, WE DON'T FACE THEM ALONE. WHEN WE STEP INTO THE UNKNOWN, WE'RE CREATING SPACE FOR JESUS TO SHOW UP.

Kristen Welch

(in)courage

A DaySpring COMMUNITY

Don't worry! God is right here with you, fighting this battle—and winning—for you. I can't wait to see how He does it!

You will not have to fight this battle. Take up your positions; stand firm and see the deliverance the Lord will give you.

II CHRONICLES 20:17 NIV

IN EVERY BATTLE WE FACE, VISIBLE OR NOT, GOD IS GIVING US THE OPPORTUNITY TO RELY SOLELY ON HIM AND WATCH THE MIRACLE WORKER IN ACTION.

Stephanie Bryant

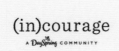

God has placed ideas in your mind and desires in your heart, and He will use them for your good and His glory. I'm praying He gives you the courage to follow His call to do just that.

*Take delight in the L*ORD*, and He will give you your heart's desires.*
PSALM 37:4 CSB

WE HAVE TO BE BRAVER THAN WE THINK WE CAN BE, BECAUSE GOD IS CONSTANTLY CALLING US TO BE MORE THAN WE ARE.

Madeleine L'Engle

I am praying for God to make you brave today, allowing you to take courage in His promises and comfort in His plans.

They will have no fear of bad news;
their hearts are steadfast,
trusting in the Lord.

PSALM 112:7 NIV

HAVING A WILLING HEART MEANS
THAT WE OBEY WITHOUT SEEING THE END
OF THE STORY, ENTRUSTING OUR WORK AND
OUR LIVES INTO THE HANDS OF THE ONE WHO
SEES THE END FROM THE BEGINNING.

Vivian Mabuni

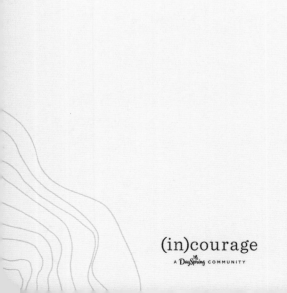

Sometimes it's easier to keep trying, to keep fighting, to keep believing we can do this on our own. I'm praying God moves in your life to allow you to see that He is fighting for you.

[God] said, "My grace is all you need. My power works best in weakness." So now I am glad to boast about my weaknesses, so that the power of Christ can work through me.... For when I am weak, then I am strong.

II CORINTHIANS 12:9-10 NLT

WEAKNESS IS A HOLY INVITATION
TO ALLOW GRACE TO DO ITS WORK.

Alia Joy

I am praying you remember everything you know to be true about God—that He is good, He loves you, His timing is perfect. And I pray that comforts you in this time.

Give all your worries and cares to God, for He cares about you.

I PETER 5:7 NLT

NEVER BE AFRAID TO TRUST AN UNKNOWN FUTURE TO A KNOWN GOD.

Corrie ten Boom

(in)courage
A DaySpring COMMUNITY

I am praying that God gives you the same faith He has in you, to show you how remarkable you are. May He give you all the courage you need and all the strength He's promised.

No, in all these things we are more than conquerors through Him who loved us.

ROMANS 8:37 CSB

HEAVEN'S LEANING OVER THE RAILS, WONDERING IF WE'LL BE AS COURAGEOUS AS GOD THINKS WE ARE.

Bob Goff

(in)courage

A DaySpring COMMUNITY

My prayer for you is complete freedom—from worry, from fear, from anxiety. I pray God gives you holy confidence that allows you to stand firm in Him and His promises.

So we say with confidence,
"The Lord is my helper; I will not be afraid.
What can mere mortals do to me?"

HEBREWS 13:6 NIV

WHEN WE FACE OUR FEARS WITH HIM, WE EXPERIENCE FREEDOM.

Jolene Underwood

Nothing can stand in the way of God's victory. Nothing! I pray you'll trust Him no matter what enemies you face, what battles you fight. God will go before you and protect you always.

The LORD is with me; I will not be afraid. What can mere mortals do to me?
PSALM 118:6 NIV

DON'T BE AFRAID OF CHANGE, BECAUSE IT IS LEADING YOU TO A NEW BEGINNING.

Joyce Meyer

Your task may be tiny and hidden, or it may be enormous and seen by all. No matter what God has called you to do, I pray He gives you the courage to do it with confidence and love.

And what does the LORD require of you? To act justly and to love mercy and to walk humbly with your God.

MICAH 6:8 NIV

COURAGE IS NOT LIMITED TO THE BATTLEFIELD OR THE INDIANAPOLIS 500 OR BRAVELY CATCHING A THIEF IN YOUR HOUSE. THE REAL TESTS OF COURAGE ARE MUCH QUIETER. THEY ARE THE INNER TESTS, LIKE REMAINING FAITHFUL WHEN NOBODY'S LOOKING, LIKE ENDURING PAIN WHEN THE ROOM IS EMPTY, LIKE STANDING ALONE WHEN YOU'RE MISUNDERSTOOD.

Charles Swindoll

Today I'm praying that you **believe** big things about our big God. May you **trust** Him to do the **impossible**, the **miraculous**, the **wondrous** work you need most in your life.

Let us then approach God's throne of grace with confidence, so that we may receive mercy and find grace to helpus in our time of need.
HEBREWS 4:16 NIV

EXPECT GREAT THINGS FROM GOD; ATTEMPT GREAT THINGS FOR GOD.
William Carey

(in)courage
A DaySpring COMMUNITY

I am praying that God will call us out into the deep waters where He is. I'm asking Him to keep our eyes on Him and hold us up as we walk toward Him and with Him.

"Come," Jesus said. So Peter went over the side of the boat and walked on the water toward Jesus.

MATTHEW 14:29 NLT

WHEN WE GET OUT OF THE BOAT AND WE KEEP OUR EYES ON JESUS, OUR FAITH WILL TAKE US PLACES WE CAN'T EVEN IMAGINE!

Jennifer Ueckert

(in)courage
A DaySpring COMMUNITY

I am praying that the Lord surrounds you with examples of **courage,** people who have faced similar circumstances and **stood firm** in the Lord. May their stories give you **strength.**

Because of my chains, most of the brothers and sisters have become confident in the Lord and dare all the more to proclaim the gospel without fear.
PHILIPPIANS 1:14 NIV

COURAGE IS CONTAGIOUS.
WHEN A BRAVE MAN TAKES A
STAND, THE SPINES OF OTHERS
ARE OFTEN STIFFENED.

Billy Graham

I am praying that God keeps drawing you near, giving you the courage you need to say yes again and again as you do the work He's created just for you.

When I am afraid, I will trust in You. In God, whose word I praise, in God I trust; I will not be afraid.

PSALM 56:3-4 CSB

OUR YES TO GOD SHOULD SCARE US. NOT TO KEEP US IMMOBILE, BUT TO KEEP US DEPENDENT ON THE ONE WHO ASKS US TO SAY IT IN THE FIRST PLACE. FEAR KEEPS US MOVING TOWARD GOD.

Kristen Welch

The Lord has given you an incredible vision, and I know He is going to do amazing things through you. I pray you lean on His strength for the courage to follow His call on your life.

*Commit to the L*ORD *whatever you do, and He will establish your plans.*
PROVERBS 16:3 NIV

CHOOSE TO SAY YES TO BIG DREAMS, EVEN WHEN FEAR IS KNOCKING AT THE DOOR.

Jessica Honegger

Worrying won't get us anywhere, so let's turn to God instead. I'm praying you can lean on Him and trust Him for what's next to come.

Who of you by worrying can add a single hour to your life?

LUKE 12:25 NIV

I DON'T KNOW HOW TO ANSWER THE "WHAT-IFS" AND "IF ONLYS" OF LIFE, BUT I KNOW THE ONE WHO CAN.

Mary Carver

God will never let you down, and you are always safe in His hands. I'm praying you'll feel comforted by His love and protection today.

Immediately they left their nets and followed Him.
MATTHEW 4:20 CSB

JESUS WANTS YOU TO SAY YES TO SURRENDERING YOUR HEART, RATHER THAN PUTTING YOUR SAFETY INTO EXECUTING A PLAN.

Bonnie Gray

Though everything feels chaotic and overwhelming, I pray you'll remember Who is in absolute control of every single speck of this universe—and I pray that comforts and encourages you.

God is our refuge and strength, an ever-present help in trouble. Therefore we will not fear, though the earth give way and the mountains fall into the heart of the sea, though its waters roar and foam and the mountains quake with their surging.

PSALM 46:1-3 NIV

IF YOU BELIEVE IN A GOD WHO CONTROLS THE BIG THINGS, YOU HAVE TO BELIEVE IN A GOD WHO CONTROLS THE LITTLE THINGS. IT IS WE, OF COURSE, TO WHOM THINGS LOOK "LITTLE" OR "BIG."

Elisabeth Elliot

Today I'm praying that you know exactly where to go with all your questions, your doubts, your fears. I pray that you give it all to the Lord, who has every answer you need.

Cast all your anxiety on Him because He cares for you.
I PETER 5:7 NIV

FAITH DOES NOT ELIMINATE QUESTIONS. BUT FAITH KNOWS WHERE TO TAKE THEM.

Elisabeth Elliot

(in)courage
A DaySpring COMMUNITY

I am praying that
God is near you today,
comforting and giving
you strength in this
difficult season.
I know He will
never leave you.

*The Lord is close to the
brokenhearted and saves those
who are crushed in spirit.*
PSALM 34:18 NIV

OUR GOD IS FAITHFUL TO STAND
BY OUR SIDE AND WALK WITH US
IN OUR DARKEST HOURS.

Adrienne Terrebonne

I pray God takes your mind off the future, relieves your heart of worries about tomorrow, and reminds you that He's in **complete control** and **provides everything** you need.

Therefore I tell you: Don't worry about your life, what you will eat or what you will drink; or about your body, what you will wear. Isn't life more than food and the body more than clothing?
MATTHEW 6:25 CSB

TOMORROW IS BUSY WORRYING ABOUT ITSELF; DON'T GET TANGLED UP IN ITS WORRY-WEBS.

Sarah Young

I know things seem bleak right now, but God is still in control. I'm praying you hold tight to your belief in Him and His good plans for you and your life.

The LORD is my light and my salvation— whom should I fear? The LORD is the stronghold of my life—whom should I dread?
PSALM 27:1 CSB

BRAVERY IS HOLDING ON TO THE FACTS OF YOUR FAITH MORE TIGHTLY HAN TO THE FEARS FOR THE FUTURE.

Kristen Strong